How to Attract the Man God Has Chosen for You

Without going on blind dates, signing up on dating websites or going to night clubs

Tamika Lane

"The longest journey begins with a single step."
—LAO-TZU

Mom
*My spiritual example, my rock and inspiration
to climb higher*

Introduction

I AM IN THE BUSINESS OF TRANSFORMING LIVES for the better. I provide women from all ethnicities, races, socioeconomic backgrounds and educational levels from all over the world the tools and principles necessary to attract the man God has chosen for them. I will assist you in gaining clarity about who you are and what you want during the dating process, so you can have a healthy, committed relationship with your soulmate. This is all accomplished from a spiritual perspective. Within this book is the information necessary to begin an individual journey towards personal alignment in achieving your greatest potential and happiness.

If you are stuck, in a rut, unsure of who you are or what your purpose is on this planet called earth, I want you to know that you are not alone. You can break free and gain insight into your destiny. You deserve the best life has to offer. The best is yet to come! In the meantime, internal work must be done to get to that place of euphoria and eternal bliss. You may ask the question, "Internal work?" Yes, internal work. Primarily work on the human mind. Yes, the brain. That complex organ above your shoulders. This is where it all begins. The mind controls every aspect of your life. When it is in alignment, great things happen and naturally unfold. When it is out of alignment, chaos, confusion, unhappiness and misery are evident and present.

I truly believe in God's plan. It is always perfect. I never doubt his plans for my life. Jeremiah 29:11 King James Version states, "For I know the thoughts that I think toward you, saith the Lord, thoughts of peace, and not of evil, to give you an expected end." I believe you are reading this right now for an expeditious plan and purpose. Maybe you have experienced hardships and difficulties in relationships in the past and are ready to try something new? Maybe you are going through something deeply personal at this very moment while reading this that is quite painful and brings you to tears? You have realized that if not now, when? You may wonder when will you experience your breakthrough? Maybe there are many things in your life that you have tried? They have not worked, and you've been left feeling frustrated, aggravated and confused.

I want you to know I have been there, and I know firsthand what desperation feels like. Just a few years ago, I was unemployed and living with my parents. My boyfriend had decided to break up with me via text message. It seemed like my life was spiraling out of control. I didn't know which way to turn or what to do. I was lonely, depressed, sad, confused and suicidal. I believed something was seriously wrong with me. Was God punishing me? Did I deserve all of this? Where is my Boaz, my soulmate, my life partner and my happily ever after?

That's when I received my breakthrough! I knew deep inside something had to change. I HAD to change. The old way of thinking had to die. Old habits, lifestyle choices and poor decisions had to die. I wanted a new way of viewing life, people and myself. I needed to be reborn and embark on a new journey to become a better, new and improved version of myself. To become the woman God wanted me to be. That was my goal. So, you know what I did? I found a quiet, comfortable place and knelt and began to pray. With tears flowing down my face, I cried out in pain and agony to God to please help me! I was broken and hurting so bad and no one knew it. I could not live the rest of my life this way. This was not an option! My desire was to be in direct alignment with what God wanted for me. That's how I knew no matter what storms blew in and no matter how hard the rain poured, I would be safe in HIS arms and under HIS wings. So, I did not worry about tomorrow. After I released all crying and pain, I felt lighter. A huge burden I had been carrying lifted off me. I felt airy. I did not have a care in the world! For the first time in a long time, I felt peaceful and it felt so good. I wanted to remain in this state for the rest of my life. This was the beginning of happiness for me. I was taking control of my life and not allowing life to take control of me!

During this process of personal alignment and breakthrough, I realized that everything I had believed up to this point wasn't true! What I had been told and groomed to believe about dating and relationships was a complete lie. It was not about signing up on countless dating websites, frequenting night clubs or going on blind dates. None of these things worked for me. Have you tried them? Have they worked for you?

You can begin the journey of attracting your soulmate. The principles introduced in my book can serve as a guide for you on your personal spiritual life, dating and relationship journey. It is a process. It takes hard work, consistency and dedication to change to become a better, new and improved version of yourself. It is worth it because only then can you reap the rewards God has in store for you! And that reward begins with a happier, healthier version of you. It all seems impossible in the beginning, yet it is very possible with God as your guide. Just stay focused and dedicated to the process. Psalm 121:1-3 King James Version states, "I will lift up mine eyes unto the hills, from whence cometh my help. My help cometh from the Lord, which made heaven and earth. He will not suffer thy foot to be moved: He that keepeth thee will not slumber." Also, Matthew 19:26 King James Version states,

"But Jesus looked at them and said to them, "With men this is impossible, but with God all things are possible."

How to Attract the Man God Has Chosen for You Copyright © 2018 by Tamika Lane.
All Rights Reserved.

All rights reserved. No part of this book may be reproduced in any form or by any electronic or mechanical means including information storage and retrieval systems, without permission in writing from the author. The only exception is by a reviewer, who may quote short excerpts in a review.

Cover designed by Tamika Lane

Printed in the United States of America

First Printing:
Kindle Direct Publishing

ISBN- 9781654200794

About the author

Author, entrepreneur, philanthropist and mentor, **Tamika Lane** is an ambitious, creative, positive soul. Her life mission is to transform other's lives through her spiritual, personal message, daily trials and triumphs. She helps women get clarity on who they are and what they want during the dating PROCESS, so they can meet their soulmate and potentially get engaged and married. She aspires to be an inspiration and light to others all over the world. She encourages women to live their best life and achieve their highest, greatest potential.

TABLE OF CONTENTS

Introduction 2
About the author 7
Author, entrepreneur, philanthropist, mentor and dating/relationship coach to women, **Tamika Lane** is an ambitious, creative, positive soul. Her life mission is to transform other's lives through her spiritual, personal message, daily trials and triumphs. She helps women get clarity on who they are and what they want during the dating PROCESS, so they can meet their soulmate and potentially get engaged and married. She aspires to be an inspiration and light to others all over the world. She encourages women to live their best life and achieve their highest, greatest potential.
.... 7
The Clarity Process: 10
Getting to Know Who You Are 10
"Knowing Yourself is the Beginning of All Wisdom" - Aristotle 10
Self-care & 13
Self-love 13
Who Is Your Higher Power? 18
Releasing Soul Ties 21
Attracting the Man 26
You Will Become the Company You Keep 30
Dating 101 33
You Have the New Relationship...Yay!!! 36
Relationship Goals 41
Biblical Relationships, Scriptures and Quotes 44

Attract the Man God Has Chosen for You

The Clarity Process: Getting to Know Who You Are

"Knowing Yourself is the Beginning of All Wisdom"-Aristotle

Knowing yourself is the beginning of all wisdom. When you know who you are and have a clear mindset of what you want, you are in the position of evoking positive change in your life. This is the foundational principle upon which everything in your life is built upon. You are an individual life force created in God's image. Acts 17:25 King James Version states, "Neither is worshipped with men's hands, as though he needed anything, seeing he giveth to all life, and breath, and all things." Romans 11:36 King James Version states, "For of Him, and through Him, and to Him, are all things: to whom be glory forever. Amen." 1 Corinthians 8:6 King James Version states, "But to us there is but one

God, the Father, of whom are all things, and we in Him; and one Lord Jesus Christ, by whom are all things, and we by Him." Every human being was created by God. Colossians 1:16 states, "For by Him were all things created, that are in heaven, and that are in earth, visible and invisible, whether they be thrones, or dominions, or principalities, or powers: all things were created by Him, and for Him." You are not an accident nor a mistake. You have been created to carry out a purpose and mission especially formulated for you. Therefore, knowing who you are is a key component to fulfilling your life's purpose. For example, can you describe who you are? Can you do a little self-analysis and really pinpoint your likes and dislikes? Your favorites, things that get on your nerves, your pet peeves? Or things that make you smile? Sad? Afraid? Worried? What do you love the most? What makes you happy? When you can sit quietly and write the answers to these questions on paper, you are on the right path. You see, most women do not know who they are or what they want whether single, dating or in a relationship. That creates a major problem going forward. You are unable to go forward, and you end up spinning your wheels going nowhere fast. This is not the plan God has for you. God's desire for you is for you to have mental clarity every day. This is the only way you can see progress in your daily life and ultimately receive true happiness and success. No one can do this for you. You must do it for yourself. So, this is what I want you to do. Purchase a journal. Take a spare moment from your busy schedule and find a quiet, comfortable spot. Using a pad and pencil (I prefer using a pencil in case I need to make updates and changes), begin brainstorming about who you are. Really, really think about this. What do you like about yourself? What do you dislike? What do you like in your life? What would you like to change? What are the deal breakers in your relationship? What are your pet peeves? What makes you angry? What makes you smile? What makes you sad? What makes you happy? What are your deepest fears? What makes you worry? What keeps you up at night? What makes you anxious? You may be able to finish in one sitting or may need more time to really think about this. The most important aspect is that you gain complete clarity on who you are as a woman. When you master knowing who you are, you are more equipped to describe yourself to others. Also, you will not allow others to tell you who you are! This is a key and very important component to establish whether single, dating or in a relationship. Ask God for help during this process. Besides, He knows all of us better than we know ourselves. I have found it personally helpful to meditate or pray before writing anything down. That way I am in my most peaceful, receptive state to hear God's voice and my own inner voice. I made the decision to do this for myself and have not looked back. It has truly made a positive difference in my life and in my professional relationships.

Self-care & Self-love

You Must First Love Yourself Before You Can Love Someone Else.

I prefer to be true to myself, even at the hazard of incurring the ridicule of others, rather than to be false, and to incur my own abhorrence."
– Frederick Douglass

Throughout the course of my life, I have realized there is nothing more important than a healthy self-esteem and the joy of loving myself. Self-care and self-love are extremely important principles in a woman's life. To be honest, in men's lives, too. When you love yourself and put yourself first, life becomes simpler and lighter. Life is not easy by no means. However, loving yourself makes the journey more bearable and easier from day to day. When you practice loving yourself, you won't beat yourself up or drag yourself down over temporary setbacks or mistakes. No one should ever want to make their own life complicated. Loving yourself gives you permission to love others. You are capable of forging healthy relationships and have more inner stability and peace. You will become oblivious to all the negativity in the world. Not naïve, just oblivious because you are focused on your goals and personal journey. Also, you are less inclined to self-sabotaging your life and relationships with others. When you can think highly of yourself and do not need validation from others, you become less needy and dependent of others. You feel more deserving of the good things in life. When God gives you those things you prayed for, you feel deserving of the bountiful blessings bestowed upon you. The opinions and feelings of others about you won't really matter. I do care about how I present myself to others, but at the beginning and end of the day, I must live with who I am and truly love myself. Therefore, I can go forward with razor sharp focus and motivation. There are many scriptural references about self-love and self-care. For example, Jeremiah 29:11 King James Version states, "For I know the thoughts that I think toward you, saith the LORD, thoughts of peace, and not of evil, to give you an expected end." 1 Peter 3:3-4 King James Version states, " Whose adorning let it not be that outward adorning of plaiting the hair, and of wearing of gold, or of putting on of apparel; But let it be the hidden man of the heart, in that which is not corruptible, even the ornament of a meek and quiet spirit, which is in the sight of God of great price. " God wants you to love yourself and take care of yourself. Looking and feeling your best on the inside is just as important as looking and feeling your best on the outside. The two go hand in hand. If your spirit is low or you are feeling down, no amount of makeup, apparel or stilettoes can make you feel or look beautiful. If you are looking tore up from the floor up, no beautiful or meek spirit can change people's perception of you. I am sure you have heard the phrase, "Don't judge a book by its cover." This is a true statement. However, one can never over nor underestimate someone by their appearance. Opening the book and getting a good understanding of the person's character is a definitive must. One of my favorite biblical scriptures to sum this up is Proverbs 4:7, "Wisdom is the principal thing; therefore, get wisdom: and with all thy getting get understanding."

∞ ∞ ∞

Our bodies are a temple. Through scripture we know that God values our bodies. Our bodies are a temple of the Holy Spirit, and we are called to take care of and honor God's temple. God's words lead use to use our bodies and the gifts He has given us to achieve His will. 1 Corinthians 6:19-20 states, "What? know ye not that your body is the temple of the Holy Ghost which is in you, which ye have of God, and ye are not your own? For ye are bought with a price: therefore, glorify God in your body, and in your spirit, which are God's." 1 Corinthians 3:16-17 states, "Know ye not that ye are the temple of God, and that the Spirit of God dwelleth in you? If any man defiles the temple of God, him shall God destroy; for the temple of God is holy, which temple ye are." Romans 12:1-2 states, "I beseech you therefore, brethren, by the mercies of God, that ye present your bodies a living sacrifice, holy, acceptable unto God, which is your reasonable service. And be not conformed to this world: but be ye transformed by the renewing of your mind, that ye may prove what is that good, and acceptable, and perfect, will of God." Matthew 6:22-23 states, "The light of the body is the eye: if therefore thine eye be single, thy whole body shall be full of light. But if thine eye be evil; thy whole body shall be full of darkness. If therefore the light that is in thee be darkness, how great is that darkness!" 1 Corinthians 10:31 states, "Whether therefore ye eat, or drink, or whatsoever ye do, do all to the glory of God." These are just a few of the amazing biblical scriptures on self-care and self-love that I truly love to read!

What we eat, drink, think, listen to and nurture our bodies with determines how we feel from day to day. It is imperative that we consume healthy foods that are nutritious and beneficial. Also, drinking adequate amounts of water daily, getting plenty of rest, relaxation, meditation and exercise are all vitally important. Incorporate spiritual practices such as meditation, yoga and bible study in your daily and weekly routine. Get daily sunlight to maintain a positive mood and spirit. Stress management is essential to a positive overall health and wellness regimen. Practice monitoring breathing and include deep breathing exercises when feeling anxious. Speak affirmations that make you feel stronger, more vibrant and excited to face your day. Practice daily gratitude for all of the people and things you are grateful for. This improves self-esteem and mood. By incorporating these activities in your daily regimen, you are sure to be on the road to improved self-esteem and self-care.

Why is a healthy self-esteem and daily self-care important while single, dating or in a relationship? When you feel your best and love yourself, you are more capable of loving the man God sends into your life. This sets the stage for a good courtship and relationship. It is impossible to have a healthy relationship and you are unhealthy. This makes no sense and the two cannot coexist! Make it a daily priority to maintain a healthy self-esteem and incorporate daily self-care practices before meeting someone new and most definitely while dating or in a relationship. You want to remain healthy and super excited about the new beginnings that lie before you!

Who Is Your Higher Power?

Who is Your God?
Do You Have One?

"Let us hear the conclusion of the whole matter: Fear God and keep his commandments: for this is the whole duty of man."
—Ecclesiastes 12:13

Who or what do you turn to when life gets hard? When things get rough? I always turn to God. He is my everything. I don't know where I would be today if He wasn't the head of my life. I surrendered all to God at age 11. And I haven't looked back. Has my life been easy? No, not at all. God never promised it would be. I still choose to trust him when times are good and when times are bad. What I do know is that if He wasn't first in my life and my top priority above everyone and everything else, my life would be very difficult. With Him serving as my guide, I know I can continue this journey no matter what comes my way. He has my back if I stick with Him. The same holds true for you, too. Who is your higher power? Do you have one? Life will throw all types of trials, tribulations and tests your way just to see what you are made of. It can leave you gasping for air and wondering what just happened. If you aren't anchored to something, you will float or fly away. Make sure you are anchored to a higher source of power and inspiration.

As a woman, you must be mindful of what you watch, whom you listen to and talk to when facing trials and tribulations in this life. Everyone is not your friend. They do not have your best interest at heart when it comes to your life and relationships. Some people will pretend to be your friend just to find out about everything going on in your life. They will go and tell others everything you just told them. They will even spread hurtful lies and rumors about you. And they call themselves your friend or brother and sister in Christ? Really? So be aware of who you share private information with. Always go to God in prayer before you reveal anything to anyone. Let holy spirit reveal to you whether this person is a trusted source.

Treat yourself with kindness and love every day. If you don't know already, God loves you! A biblical scripture I truly love to read is John 3:16-17 King James Version, "For God so loved the world that he gave his only begotten Son, that whosoever believeth in Him should not perish, but have everlasting life." That means the world to me! If I just believe and trust in God, I can have everlasting life. Always remember to treat not just yourself with kindness and love but others also. Even if you feel deep down inside that they don't deserve it. I believe in karma.

Always pray and develop a daily prayerful, purposeful life. Develop and maintain a deep relationship with God (Higher Power). Study God's word daily. Pray to God for the power of supernatural spiritual discernment. This is important and valuable in your dating life and lifetime relationships. Psalm 47:2 King James Version states. "For the Lord most high is terrible; He is a great King over all the earth." Develop a lifetime relationship with God and watch your life miraculously change in more positive ways than you could ever imagine!

God will lead you every step of the way. It is important for you to have a rock-solid relationship with Him, so you can be ready for a healthy, committed dating life, relationship and marriage where God is the head.

Releasing Soul Ties
How to Release Them

"Flee fornication. Every sin that a man doeth is without the body; but he that committeth fornication sinneth against his own body."
—*1 Corinthians 6:18*

Release those ties from former lovers. What are soul ties? Soul ties are intimate, sexual relationships one has developed with someone. It may even be a mental bond with someone that has developed over months or even years. Maybe you left them and have begun a new relationship? Maybe you know you shouldn't be with them but cannot break free and completely leave them? Maybe you were in an intimate relationship with someone and want to break free to please God but don't know how? All soul ties are not bad. God created each one of us to form bonds with other people. If the bond or relationship is something God ordained, and He wants you to be with this person and communicate with them, then the soul tie is not bad at all. It is divine intervention and God's will for you to be together. However, other relationships that God never wanted you to be in and He has wanted you to sever that relationship for the last few months or years and you can't seem to let it go, then that is a soul tie that needs to be broken. Matthew 18:19 King James Version states "Again I say unto you, that if two of you shall agree on earth as touching anything that they shall ask, it shall be done for them of my Father which is in heaven. If two of you shall ask, it shall be done for them." When two people come together under this circumstance, God's power is strengthened in this bond. Mark 10:8 King James Version states, "And they twain shall be one flesh: so, then they are no more twain, but one flesh." People come into our lives for many different reasons. I will give you some examples. Close relationships can form with people you choose to spend a lot of time with. Whether traveling, eating, talking, working together, the bond can grow over time. You can have soul ties with family members, children, friends and even coworkers. It is not always a sexual bond. 1 Samuel 18:1 King James Version speaks about the kinship between Jonathan and David. "And it came to pass, when he had made an end of speaking to Saul, that the soul of Jonathan was knit with the soul of David, and Jonathan loved him as his own soul." This is an example of a soul tie bond between two men who were spiritually connected and close friends. However, when God has not ordained the soul tie, Satan can enter this situation and his evil deeds and powers can intensify. Another example is when we make promises to others and offer commitments. The words spoken from one person to another forms a soul tie. Our words are very powerful. For example, the following statements hold tremendous power: "I hate you!", "I will always love you.", "No one will ever take your place." "You are the only one for me." Proverbs 6:2 King James Version states. "Thou art snared with the words of thy mouth, thou art taken with the words of thy mouth." A snare is a trap that can hold you hostage in one place and prevent you from moving forward. Another example is in sexual relationships. We have all been there. These soul ties form when there is intimacy in a relationship. You may have ended the relationship for months or years but still feel a pull towards a particular person. That is a soul tie. Soul ties can keep you from moving from a bad relationship to one God has chosen for you to be in. It can happen due to divorce. One ex-spouse has moved one but the other keeps being drawn back to their former ex. Their soul is tied to their ex-husband or ex-wife. James 1:8 King James Version states." A double minded man is unstable in all his ways." A double minded person has a divided soul. Have you ever felt unstable? Double-minded? This is not what God wants for you. He wants you free from every sin of your past. Even ones you willingly gave into. There are things you can do to break free. Choose to please God over man. If you choose to do otherwise, you will find your life spinning out of control. Your life will be filled with regret. Time does not stand still for anyone. Years wasted can never be replaced. Each of us are aging every second of every day. We must be aware of how we spend our time and who we choose to spend it with. Has God prompted you to end an unhealthy relationship? Listen to God and end it. When we disobey God, there are consequences to our actions. Disobedience allows Satan to enter and he will keep you locked into an unhealthy situation for a lifetime. That is his job. To kill and destroy. Don't let Satan rob you of your life, health and joy. Follow God and obey His voice instead. You will never regret it. I speak on the importance of studying God's word every day because I know from personal experience that it is powerful stuff! Hebrews 4:12 King James Version states, "For the word of God is quick, and powerful, and sharper than any two-edged sword, piercing even to the dividing asunder of soul and spirit, and of the joints and marrow, and is a discerner of the thoughts and intents of the heart." This scripture alone is so powerful! You need God's word to help you break free of soul ties. There is nothing God cannot do. Prayer changes things! I am a witness. Pray to God to help you release this person from your mind, body, soul and spirit and He will help you. You must ask Him for help. Satan will come to you in dreams, visions and messages to try to deceive and convince you why you should stay with this person or maintain the bond. It is all lies. Don't fall for it! Grow closer to God each day by staying in His word so He can guide you and free you. Breaking ungodly soul ties is not easy to do. You must gradually wean yourself from this person. It can be done. I had to wean myself from a boyfriend from my past. Psalm 131:2 King James Version states, "Surely I have calmed and quieted my soul like a weaned child with his mother. Like a weaned child is my soul within me ceased from fretting." The word fretting means worrying. Worry leads to anxiety. When we have an ungodly soul tie, our soul is not at peace. It is in a state of fretting and worrying. It appears that it is the right thing when in fact is truly isn't. It is never easy weaning oneself from someone or something we desire. It is like taking a toy from a baby. The baby may throw a fit and cry, kick and scream all day and all night. You may even cry and scream and throw a fit. Rest assured, this too shall pass. Just stick with it. Each day will get a little easier. John 14:23 King James Version states, "Jesus answered and said unto him, if a man loves me, he will keep my words: and my Father will love him, and we will come unto him and make our abode with him."

Attract the Man God Has Chosen for You

Attracting the Man

Where Is Your Boaz?

*"Delight thyself also in the Lord;
and He shall give thee the desires of
thine heart."*
—*Psalm 37:4*

What type of man do you seek to attract? This is an important question to consider while dating. The type of energy you put out will most definitely return unto you. That is the type of man you will attract. Are you a negative person? Do you expect the worst to happen? If so, it will most definitely manifest its ugly self into your life and turn your world upside down. Do you expect the best to happen? Are you a positive woman and expect the best? Sure, you may have some hills and valleys and everything in between, but rest assured the best outcome will present itself in due time. Proverbs 3:3-6 King James Version states, "Whose adorning let it not be that outward (adorning) of plaiting the hair, and of wearing of gold, or of putting on apparel; but let it be the hidden man of the heart, in that which is not corruptible, (even the ornament) of a meek and quiet spirit, which is in the sight of God of great price. For after this manner in the old time the holy women also, who trusted in God, adorned themselves, being in subjection unto their own husbands: Even as Sara obeyed Abraham, calling him lord; whose daughters ye are, as long as ye do well, and are not afraid with any amazement." I know times have changed since the biblical days. A woman should dress well and look her best. She will attract men to her by her appearance alone. But the goal is not to attract ALL men, just the one God has chosen for you. You will turn many heads wearing high heels and short skirts but also attract the wrong attention. Be mindful of how you dress so you do not attract the wrong attention. Dress in ways that are classy and sophisticated. Give men the illusion of sexiness and much to be desired by not revealing too much of yourself. It is okay to be sexy but do it in a classy, sophisticated way. Dresses and skirts do not have to be down to your ankles and blouses buttoned all the way up to the top of your neck for you to be called a Christian or a spiritual woman. If that is your thing to dress this way, do what makes you happy. Just remember, it is about your relationship with God that determines your destiny. Sometimes we try to overcomplicate the dating and relationship process by putting a lot of rules and regulations on everything. It is not complicated and not rocket science. It is two different people coming together and deciding that they want to get to know more about each other. That's it! I will share a secret with you. You must first develop into the woman or at least be on the journey in developing into her before God will allow you to attract the man, he has chosen for you. If you are out here playing games, playing the field, running from pillar to post, you might as well just sit down. God will never send the man he desires for you to be with while you are in that state of mind. Your life will get better when you get better. That is a fact! God wants you to be a whole woman, so you can attract a whole man. It is never your responsibility to make a man whole or try to fix and man. It is not his responsibility to make you whole or try to fix you either. That is not God's plan. Though I see many men and women in roles God has not designed. It is making them miserable, too. Remember when I said it all begins with your mindset. If you focus everyday cultivating positive thoughts, you will attract positive people and situations into your life. If you spend your time focusing on cultivating negative thoughts, you will indeed attract negative people and situations into your life. I know personally that this is not always easy to do. Our minds are bombarded with so much information and unlimited distractions. It is doable and possible to be a positive person. Consistency is the key. You must practice at it every day. There are no shortcuts! Even when you practice cultivating positive thoughts daily, you will have some difficult days and nights and by no means will the road always be smooth. Let God sort all of that out. Just do your part and He will handle the rest.

∞ ∞ ∞

If you meet someone, how will you know he is the one? I will tell you, when you pray about it and talk to God, He will reveal this to you. He will reveal the thoughts and intentions of others to you. That is why it is so important for you to have a true, transparent relationship with God. You want to be in the best possible position with God, so you are always able to hear his voice. Be very still and silent so you can hear him when He speaks. The holy spirit will reveal the innermost thoughts and feelings of your heart and the thoughts and intentions of the one you are interested in. Tell God exactly what you desire. Be very specific in your prayers and if it is His will, He will give you the desires of your heart. It is His will that you live your best life. A life filled with abundance and prosperity. Matthew 7:7 states, "Ask, and it shall be given you; seek, and you will find. knock, and the door will be opened to you. "

You Will Become the Company You Keep

"Be not deceived: evil communications corrupt good manners."
—*1 Corinthians 15:33*

Keep yourself from diverse temptations. Evil communication corrupts good morals. This is a true biblical scripture that still applies today. Be very conscious and aware of the company you keep. Whether single, dating, in a committed relationship or marriage. Your company will affect you and therefore will affect the outcome of your situation. I cannot tell you how many people I know who have allowed family members, friends, associates, coworkers and even their closest confidantes affect their relationships. I will even go as far to say even their marriage. If the advice received is good and benefits you, then continue to receive it. Make sure the individual or individuals you communicate with do not have an ulterior motive. Know your company and their background. Once the information is out there, you cannot get it back. You don't want people you never intended to partake of your information to receive it and gossip about it. That can prove to be very devastating and hurtful. Maybe you have reached a time in your life where some friendships must end. You have outgrown them and must progress forward with your life. There is nothing wrong with that. Do what is best for you. Don't allow others who do not know you or have your best interest at heart control your life. Those who love you, will allow you to grow and become the best version of you. They will tell you when you are wrong and give you the best advice. Those with ulterior motives will never give you the best advice and will always seek to see you hurt and devastated. They will pretend to want what is best for you. 1 Peter 5:8 King James Version states, "Be sober, be vigilant; because your adversary the devil, as a roaring lion, walketh about seeking whom he may devour." How you begin your dating life, or your relationship always sets the stage for how it will be. It can either improve or become worse. Always carry yourself with dignity and respect. Demand respect always. Respect is earned, not given. This applies to men, too. Avoid toxic relationships, including those of your closest family members. Keep yourself from environments that will give you a bad reputation and label you as someone with poor character. People will label you by the places you visit, the company you keep and by your character. No man wants to be with a woman who makes poor decisions and choices. No woman should want to be with a man who does the same. Be with someone who represents themselves well and is a good judge of character. A man with a good head on his shoulders should be a goal. Anything less than this is not God's will. Therefore, you will not meet the man God has chosen for you if you are behaving unjustly or living your life under unholy circumstances. Your goal is for a man to see you as a woman of God! Nothing less. So, if you are living your life in ways that are unbecoming, you will never meet the man God has chosen for you. It will never happen! Keep yourself free from evil temptation and evil communication. Sit back and see how making better decisions affects your dating life and relationships in a very positive, beneficial way.

Dating 101

The Interview Process

"Be ye not unequally yoked together with unbelievers: for what fellowship hath righteousness with unrighteousness? And what communion hath light with darkness?"

—2 Corinthians 6:14

Be equally yoked. This means being compatible on a spiritual and relationship level. So, you have met someone you really like and perhaps would like to date. That is wonderful! There are some key pieces of information you must keep in mind. First, keep yourself focused and your emotions under control. Maintain self-control. Second, remain analytical after you meet them. Keep your eyes and ears always open. You are getting to know them, but don't really know them at all. Do not behave as if you know them or have known them all your life. There may be chemistry between the two of you, but it takes time to really get to know someone. The process cannot be rushed, no matter how cute he is, how much he has to offer you or how much you love his smile. Slow down and treat this as an interview. Ask questions, questions and more questions. Do not get touchy, feely with him. Don't allow him to do this to you either. Set up boundaries and keep them up. You must respect yourself and make sure he respects you. The man God has chosen for you will know how to respect you and will treat you like a queen. Make sure you are being transparent with him, so he knows exactly what you want and expect. Take notes during conversations, in person, over the phone or via Skype or email. Refer to your notes as necessary to draw conclusions about anything he has said or mentioned. Tell him about your dating and relationship goals. If you want to one day get married and have kids, ask him if he wants the same. It would be a waste of time at this point if he does not want the same things as you do. So, ask plenty of questions. If you are dating, it is most imperative to ask clear, concise questions. Whether dating, in a relationship or married, make sure you always keep the lines of communication open. Make sure you and he are always on the same page to avoid misunderstandings and miscommunications.

Communication is key. With our busy lives and schedules, it is so easy to forget to adequately and properly communicate in ways that are beneficial for both parties and truly effective. Keep these points in mind and you will be sailing ahead with confidence, fully aware of who you are and what you desire your relationship to be.

You Have the New Relationship...Yay!!!

How Will You Make It Last?

> "Be confident of this very thing, that he which hath begun a good work in you will perform it until the day of Jesus Christ."
> —*Philippians 1:6*

You have met your soulmate. I am excited for you! You have put a lot of hard work in yourself and have prepared for this special time. It is what you prayed for! God has FINALLY answered your prayers. God will not bring you to a thing to leave you stranded. This is the man He has chosen for you. If you remain close to God, He will make sure your relationship lasts.

How will you maintain the new relationship? It took some time and even work for you to get here. Maintaining the relationship is your goal so you can get engaged and married. Staying close to God is the key to making any relationship last! Pray with your new partner, in season and out of season. Make sure you are on the same page in the relationship. People change over time, in various ways. Make sure you are growing together and are not growing apart. So, it is imperative that you always communicate your goals, hopes and dreams with your partner. Let them know what is working for you and even what you would like to see change and improve. Always pray to God before speaking with them. Let the holy spirit guide you. Never use condescending language or point blame. This only leads to hurt feelings and disappointment. Use kind words and speak with love. You will most definitely get the results you desire and will communicate and get meaningful results in your new relationship. All relationships take work. There will be obstacles. That is life. It is not always easy. However, with the right strategies, your relationship can and will last. I always like to reiterate that all relationships are two imperfect people coming together to make something as close to perfect as they possibly can. No one is perfect! It baffles me why more couples do not realize this. Yet unrealistic expectations are constantly placed on each other daily, creating resentment and unnecessary pressures. We must stop this! Working together as a team is something all couples must do. Growth is a process. It will not happen overnight. Have you ever seen a baby grow into an adult overnight? Your new partner may have flaws and quirks that get on your last nerve. And you may have your own flaws and quirks that get on his last nerve. One should never throw away a relationship over differences. We are all different. This is how God created us. If He wanted us to be the same, we all would be. Let's embrace the differences in each of us, especially in a new relationship. Don't give up on each other but hang in there and work through the differences. You are bringing new ideas, tactics, ways of thinking and solving problems in the relationship. He is bringing his own ways of thinking and doing things. Somewhere in the middle the two of you can meet and something unique and different can be birthed that can benefit both of you. When God sent you this man, He created him just for you. He never promised you he would be perfect. I am sure the man you have attracted was expecting someone different. Being a whole person does not mean perfection. The truth is God never makes a mistake. We may not understand His thoughts and intentions, but He knows exactly what He is doing. We must trust Him. Isaiah 55:8-9 King James Version states, "For my thoughts are not your thoughts, neither are your ways my ways, declares the Lord. As the heavens are higher than the earth, so are my ways higher than your ways and my thoughts than your thoughts." Healthy communication is key. You will grow and change every single day and so will your partner. Grow together and change for the better. Always move forward. Love unconditionally. Laugh and have fun together. Learn to laugh at yourself. Enjoy life for it passes by so quickly. Don't dwell on the petty, small things of life. Focus on the bigger picture. Enjoy the journey. It is a journey, not a sprint to the finish line. The beginning stages of falling in love are magical, new, and refreshing. Everything else in life seems to stop as you move through time. It feels as though you've found the one who knows your soul inside and out. Don't be alarmed if as the months and years pass, this new feeling seems to dissipate. You start to wonder if it was all in your imagination. Is this love real? Why don't I feel the same about him and him about me? In most cases, the love is very real. Problems arise when one or both of you stop adding more to the relationship to keep it fresh and invigorating. One person cannot do it all to maintain a healthy, committed relationship. It takes both constantly adding to it to keep it nourished. It is like adding water to a well or water to a pot on the stove. If the heat is high, eventually the water will boil, steam will dissipate, and the pot will even burn if the stove is not turned off. Nourishment, in every aspect, provides the soul with fulfillment and feeds that feeling of love. In the beginning of a relationship this happens almost involuntarily as you and your love will glow and thrive in this new love affair. You feel, interpret, and process the spiritual aspects of each other without much consideration. As life settles in and the initial high of a new relationship wears off, it becomes more difficult to maintain the vitality of your relationship. The world didn't stop when you fell in love; love just became the focus. When that focus settles back on the day to day, you need to work harder to honor your relationship. To find the right balance of romance, spirituality, respect, trust, and unity, there are strategies that can be implemented. Cultivate loving habits with each other daily. For example, in the morning greet by sending them a good morning text or call. This means a lot in starting your day off right. Do as much as you can throughout your day together. Share stories of your time apart. Although not a shared experience, the conversation gives the feeling of less separation and more honesty. Make sure your energy (aura) is good. Other people can feel the auric energy field around you, and you can intentionally give that energy to another person. To give the right energy to your partner, the trick is to connect with what was natural in the beginning. Make it a point to show your love in some way, be it big or small, every day. It can be in the form of a hug, a thoughtful word, or a small gift. These gestures keep your mutual attention on your relationship and this combined energy and focus is very healthy. It's important to recognize the common interests of your relationship. What do you enjoy doing together? In the process, you can find yourselves in each other. Cultivate your common life focuses and learn to see yourselves as a unit with a shared consciousness or common identity. Your shared focuses can be the well-being of the relationship, a mutual business or career, or other common goals. Ask yourselves a few simple questions to help explore this concept.

- What aspects of life are most important?
- What are your common goals and interests?
- What activities did you enjoy when life was just about sharing time with each other?

It is imperative that we take thoughtful steps back from our busy lives to focus on what is really, truly most important. The people closest to us is what matters most. Be it a new relationship, family or friends. We tend to focus most on those things or people that mean the most to us. Maintaining your relationship must be your shared focus to ensure you have a healthy beginning and reach your goal of getting that marriage proposal and also planning your dream wedding. The work on the relationship must continue after the proposal and especially after the words "I DO" are uttered at the wedding. Keep God first and give your new relationship the love and attention it deserves. Water it daily and watch it grow!

Relationship Goals

What are your relationship goals?

"It takes three to make love, not two: you, your spouse, and God. Without God people only succeed in bringing out the worst in one another. Lovers who have nothing else to do but love each other soon find there is nothing else. Without a central loyalty life is unfinished. "- Fulton J. Sheen

What are your relationship goals? What does your future look like with your new partner? Do you desire to have children? Adopt children? Get married? Elope? Travel the world together? Be a stay at home parent? Work from home? Start a business together? The list goes on and on. I am sure you can come up with a list of questions to ask him. Make sure you do and ensure you want the same things. There is nothing worse than a couple with two different life viewpoints and goals. This is a recipe for disaster. It doesn't have to be. Designate some time for the two of you to come together and communicate your goals for the relationship. Do this at least every 3 months. Check in with each other and ask the important questions so you both know where your future is headed. After all, you are in this together. If you realize on certain topics you don't want the same things, how much are one or both of you willing to compromise? Sometimes we must be willing to compromise to have a healthy relationship. Vulnerability does not mean weakness. Be vulnerable and transparent with your partner. They are sure to love and appreciate you more. The "my way or it's the highway" mentality will not work and only creates an acrimonious affair. I am sure that is not one of your relationship goals. So be clear with each other on what you both want in a tactful, loving way. Choose to be happy together. I've learned in my personal relationship to be happy alone and when with my partner. It has really served me well. It has created more balance in the relationship. My happiness is not dependent on being around him. And his happiness is not dependent on being around me. We complement each other. When we are together and spend time doing things together, the relationship is enhanced. We realize we are two, different human beings living two, separate lives. Autonomy is important. We choose to be happy together yet not lose ourselves in each other. We also focus on doing something fun and exciting at least once a month. Be it going to see a new movie, trying out a new restaurant or traveling to a new city. This is our time to enjoy life together. It is our idea of fun, no matter what is. Carve out time to do fun things together, based on your individual schedules and availability. Focus on the positive. Remember why you fell in love in the first place. You may have disagreements and argue, and that is completely normal. If anyone tells you they never have disagreements in their relationship, they are lying to you. Couples often get lost focusing on the negatives instead of the positives. That is unhealthy for both of you. Always remember why you love each other and focus on the positives. Schedule date nights. It doesn't have to be an elaborate affair. Just the two of you going somewhere together to enjoy each other's company. Find causes you both are passionate about and volunteer or give back to others. Show your respect and appreciation for each other every day. Say phrases like "thank you", "I love you" and "I'm grateful for you" to let your partner know how much you care for them. Most often women feel unappreciated in relationships. I have learned that there are times when men feel the exact same way. So, it is equally important to show gratitude and appreciation for each other. There will be times when you or your partner will set individual goals. Show your support to them whether it is a career change or a choice to go back to school. Make sure they are supporting you in your endeavors as well. This will make you a stronger couple. Stay focused and committed to attaining your relationship goals! You will be so glad you did!

Biblical Relationships, Scriptures and Quotes

"But seek ye first the kingdom of God, and his righteousness; and all these things shall be added unto you." -Matthew 6:33

I choose to marry a man who loves God more than he loves me. This is my personal goal. And I know when the time is right, it will become my reality. The next few sentences, biblical scriptures and quotes represent inspirational messages that will guide you on your journey of growth and spiritual enlightenment. Enjoy!!!

You ought to marry someone who's willing to go anywhere for God. If they're not, they're out. - John Piper

A man who will lead you to God and not to sin is worth waiting for.

A relationship that lasts is one with God in the center.

If God is the center of your relationship nothing can break it.

It's about trusting in one another and trusting in God's plan, that He will build your relationship into one that will last a lifetime.

The closer we move toward God, the closer we move toward each other.

God is writing your love story. Let Him read it to you.

Always pray for your partner to be in love with God more than yourself. A God-centered relationship is always honorable and more likely to be a blessing.

Imagine a man/woman so focused on God that the only reason she/he looked up to see you is because she/he heard God say: "There she/he is".

A relationship where you can pray, worship and passionately pursue God together is always worth having.

God, Him and Her! A cord of three strands is not easily broken.

The right relationship won't distract you from God. It will bring you closer to Him.

A God-centered Home is a home where God is on the throne. It's a home that thanks God for the High and Lows. Where God is called on to give purpose, comfort and direction.

How do you make God the center of your relationship? The simplest answer would be to make sure that you're both pursuing God more than you're pursuing each other.

My prayer is that people see God in us and our relationship.

A happy marriage is not the goal. It is the inevitable fruit of a God-centered relationship.

Nowadays relationships last 'till whenever, but when God is involved, they last forever.

Purity is attractive. Not only does it show self-worth and self-respect, but it also shows reverence and obedience to God.

For a relationship to truly last forever, both people need to put God first before anything in their lives.

A real man doesn't put his woman first. A real man puts God first, because he knows that he must follow God in order to lead his lady.

Godly relationships don't just happen. They take two people who are committed to putting God first and the willingness to face anything together.

Date someone who will chase God with you.

Be with someone who makes you fall more in love with God every day.

Focus on becoming the right person instead of finding the right person

Titus 2:2-8

That the aged men be sober, grave, temperate, sound in faith, in charity, in patience.

The aged women likewise, that they be in behaviour as becometh holiness, not false accusers, not given to much wine, teachers of good things;

That they may teach the young women to be sober, to love their husbands, to love their children,

To be discreet, chaste, keepers at home, good, obedient to their own husbands, that the word of God be not blasphemed.

Young men likewise exhort to be sober minded.

In all things shewing thyself a pattern of good works: in doctrine shewing uncorruptness, gravity, sincerity,

Sound speech, that cannot be condemned; that he that is of the contrary part may be ashamed, having no evil thing to say of you.

Submit your life and relationship to God

Proverbs 15:22

Without counsel purposes are disappointed: but in the multitude of counsellors they are established.

Be happy with God first

Psalm 84:11

For the Lord God is a sun and shield: The Lord will give grace and glory: no good thing will he withhold from them that walk uprightly.

Men should lead by example and women should complement

Submitting yourselves one to another in the fear of God.
Wives, submit yourselves unto your own husbands, as unto the Lord.
For the husband is the head of the wife, even as Christ is the head of the church: and he is the saviour of the body.

Therefore as the church is subject unto Christ, so let the wives be to their own husbands in everything.
Husbands, love your wives, even as Christ also loved the church, and gave himself for it;

Commit yourself to your wife/husband

1 Corinthians 13:4-8

Charity suffereth long, and is kind; charity envieth not; charity vaunteth not itself, is not puffed up,
Doth not behave itself unseemly, seeketh not her own, is not easily provoked, thinketh no evil;
Rejoiceth not in iniquity, but rejoiceth in the truth;
Beareth all things, believeth all things, hopeth all things, endureth all things.
Charity never faileth: but whether there be prophecies, they shall fail; whether there be tongues, they shall cease; whether there be knowledge, it shall vanish away.

Learn to communicate

Ephesians 4:25-29

Wherefore putting away lying, speak every man truth with his neighbour: for we are members one of another.
Be ye angry, and sin not: let not the sun go down upon your wrath:
Neither give place to the devil.

Let him that stole steal no more: but rather let him labour, working with his hands the thing which is good, that he may have to give to him that needeth.

My relationship with God is my number one focus. I know that if I take care of that, God will take care of everything else.

The way I see it, putting your faith in God is something that each person has gotta come to on his or her own. It's your own personal relationship with Him; a bond that's as unique as a fingerprint. - Bethany Hamilton

Faith is the gaze of a soul upon a saving God. - A.W. Tozer

God wants us to humbly and sincerely ask Him things. How often do you enjoy people talking about you without taking the time to get to know you? - Criss Jami

Nothing teaches us about the preciousness of the Creator as much as when we learn the emptiness of everything else. - Charles Spurgeon

It's bad enough for me to make choices that hurt my own relationship with God. How much more serious is it to be the cause of someone else deciding to sin? Not only must I choose the pathway of holiness for God's sake and for my own sake; I must also do it for the sake of others. - Nancy Leigh DeMoss

Our relationship must be right with God before it can be right with man. - Billy Graham

Some people think God does not like to be troubled with our constant coming and asking. The way to trouble God is not to come at all. - D.L. Moody

Even if you have got nothing else left, be proud of your relationship with God. - Sunday Adelaja

Loving the world destroys our relationship with God, it denies our faith in God, and it discounts our future with God. - David Jeremiah

Be in a close association with your creator whose is ever ready to direct your plans. Always ensure your convictions are divine and backed by a Godly approval. - Israelmore Ayivor

Money can come and go, and fame comes and goes. Peace of mind and a relationship with God is far more important, so this is the precedent that we've set in our lives. The bottom line is, we all die, so Jesus is the answer. - Phil Robertson

Let no corrupt communication proceed out of your mouth, but that which is good to the use of edifying, that it may minister grace unto the hearers.

My highest mission and goal in writing this book is for it to inspire you to think and have a sustained hope for a brighter tomorrow. Everything that has been written I have experienced and have applied to my own life and relationship. I am a work in progress. Each day I desire to do better than I did the day before. I pray you have gained insight into who you are as a woman on your spiritual journey and have gained more clarity on what it takes to attract the man God has chosen for you. You now have a good foundation to plant seeds that are necessary to really make your relationship meaningful! Remember to put God first, nourish yourself and your relationship. Sit back and watch it grow!

Thanks for reading! If you enjoyed this book or found it to be useful, I would be very grateful if you would post a short review on www.Amazon.com. Your support really does make a difference. I read the reviews personally, so I can get your feedback and make this book even better. Thanks again for your support!

Tamika Lane

Tamika Lane

∞ ∞ ∞

Tamika Lane